AIR FRYER
COOKBOOK

Easy **Air Fryer** Recipes for Fast,
Healthy & Delicious Meals

Published by The Fruitful Mind LTD.

Disclaimer

The information in this book is not to be used as medical advice. The recipes should be used in combination with guidance from your physician. Please consult your physician before beginning any diet. It is especially important for those with diabetes, and those on medications to consult with their physician before making changes to their diet.

Disclaimer and Terms of Use: Effort has been made to ensure that the information in this book is accurate and complete, however, the author and the publisher do not warrant the accuracy of the information, text and graphics contained within the book due to the rapidly changing nature of science, research, known and unknown facts and internet. The Author and the publisher do not hold any responsibility for errors, omissions or contrary interpretation of tahe subject matter herein. This book is presented solely for motivational and informational purposes only.

Special Gifts For Readers

As a reader of this book, you can get free access to other bonuses from The Fruitful Mind, including:

- 40 Healthy Habits Wellness Guide

- Fast Metabolism Secrets PDF Report

- Free & Discounted #1 Bestselling Health eBooks

And much more that will help you lose weight, increase energy and feel great! To get these free bonuses, please visit:

www.thefruitfulmind.com

Introduction

For those of us with a constant hankering for French fries, fried chicken, and other, greasy, gut-bombs, the Air Fryer is a dream appliance. It allows you to re-create these glorious meals, along with countless others, in a fresher, much healthier way—without unnecessary fat, and without that nasty grease smell that would, inevitably, make your kitchen, house, and dog reek for all of eternity. Thank goodness. Your pillows are saved.

In fact, the Air Fryer uses up to 80% less oil than other fryers, thus cooking your food with hot "air" (as the name suggests), which—if you haven't checked lately—doesn't have a single calorie in it. Amazing.

In this book, you'll discover the incredible benefits of the Air Fryer, just why it's so easy to clean, tips and tricks for best utilization, and safety tips.

Beyond that, you'll dive into the many breakfast recipes—from breakfast burritos and sandwiches to frittatas, to chicken and fish recipes, including Sweet and Sour Chicken and Crunchy Coconut Shrimp. The beef and pork chapter offers some normal gut-bombs, like burgers and pork belly, but without the typical time blocks—and without any unnecessary calories. Many of these recipes are also high-protein, ketogenic-friendly, thus allowing you to keep track of your carbs and lose some weight.

As you'll learn in this book, the Air Fryer cooks faster, and more safely, than the oven or the stove. All you need to do is set the timer, be around to flip and shake every once in a while, and remove your food when the timer blares. Easy enough.

Good luck on this journey of weight loss, discovery, and extra time. Who knows what you'll do with that extra hour every evening, when you'd normally be slaving over a stove? Perhaps you'll pick up a hobby. Perhaps you'll cure a major world illness. Or, perhaps, you'll just get some much-needed shuteye. Your call.

Table of Contents

Chapter 1: Benefits, Safety, and Tips for Best Air Fryer Use

The Air Fryer is a "dream" appliance, and one of the most talked about new items on the marketplace right now. And, like your brave cooking forefathers before you, you've decided to make the leap and opt for this new, trendy Fryer. You're confident and ready to enjoy delicious, healthy food. Who can blame you?

After all, Air Fryers have a ton to offer. They allow for easy clean up, very low-fat meals, utilization of many different ingredients, which can be cooked at all angles with the circulating air (and without oil!), all while sparing your home of those unnecessary and gross "fried" smells.

Benefits of the Air Fryer: An Appliance You Won't Know How You Lived Without

The Air Fryer was cultivated in England in 2008, a place that suffered with an obesity epidemic due to its hearty appetite for fried foods, like fish and chips. The appliance allows you to bake, cook, fry, grill, and steam foods. As you can imagine, it didn't take long for the rest of the world to catch on.

The Air Fryer contains a frying basket, a heating element, along with an under pan that catches the dripping fat (allowing for easy cleanup). As the food cooks, the heating element ensures that the exterior of your food is crispy, and the interior of your food is tender and well-cooked. Just like you like it.

According to in-depth nutritional research, Air Frying is much better for your health, as much of the food is cooked without added oils and fats. As a result, when compared to other fryers, its food has up to 80 percent less fat. This can mean the difference between obesity and feeling confident, healthy, and strong.

Furthermore, with the Air Fryer, you can remain on your healthy, wholesome diet, all within the terrible time constraints of your schedule. Most of the recipes in this book can be made in 30 minutes or less. As an example, French fries can be fried up in the Air Fryer in about 12 minutes. And let's not even discuss a prime steak, which can be dished out to you so much quicker than normal, resulting in a spontaneous, delicious evening.

Generally speaking, the Air Fryer eliminates about 50% of your cooking time, meaning you can attend to your other household chores, or just get a much-needed nap with the time you save.

Tips and Tricks for Air Frying

In my experience, heating the fryer for approximately three minutes prior to cooking anything allows for best results, similar to any skillet you've worked with in the past. However, preheating is not ALWAYS required, and I will mention if it is throughout this recipe book.

Furthermore, if you brush a tiny amount of oil or butter upon the surface of the Air Fryer—without going overboard, of course—your results will be crispier and more golden, resulting in a better overall flavor.

When cooking almost anything in the Air Fryer, including fried chicken, French fries, steaks, and burgers, it's generally important to flip the items so that they won't stick to the bottom. Furthermore, shaking the Fries and other items as they cook allows for them to maintain their crispiness, and further ensures they don't stick to each other. For best results, try to do this shaking or flipping every 10 or five minutes.

Also, when cooking, make sure that you pat foods dry before cooking them in the Air Fryer. For example, if you marinate some chicken, try to remember to pat it dry to ensure that the marinade doesn't splatter and make a bigger mess than necessary. Furthermore, after cooking foods with higher fat content, always empty out the fat from the bottom tray.

If you want to cook pre-made packaged food (not always the healthiest, but we all get hungry and behind on our schedules) always make the Air Fryer temperature about 100 degrees lower than the listed oven temperature. Reduce the cooking time by about half. This will vary based on what kinds of foods you are making. Pay attention so as not to burn them.

In order to clean up after yourself, just remove the basket from the Air Fryer and soak it in a bit of hot water.

Safety Precautions

The Air Fryer is one of the safest appliances in your kitchen, as long as you know how to use it properly.

Naturally, it's essential that you don't clean or rinse the electrical components of the Air Fryer, which can ultimately result in short circuiting and shocks.

Also, it's discouraged to fill the pan with oil, as the Air Fryer is made to work without them. Throughout this book, a recipe might require a small bit of oil. But ensure that you don't overdo it, as this can be detrimental to both the appliance and your health.

Furthermore, prior to cleaning the Air Fryer, you should always wait at least 30 minutes for it to cool after use. When the Air Fryer is hot, it is very important that you don't touch the inside of the appliance.

For best results, pay attention to your reader's manual, and follow any and all instructions carefully. Keep the Air Fryer clean between uses, and always be careful when opening the Air Fryer, as the steam that escapes can be quite hot. In the next section, we'll get started with the most important meal of the day: breakfast!

AIR FRYER
BREAKFAST RECIPES

DELIRIOUSLY DELICIOUS FRENCH TOAST STICKS

Recipe Makes 2 Servings.

Preparation Time: 18 minutes

Nutritional Information Per Serving: 244 calories, 10 grams carbohydrates, 19 grams fat, 7 grams protein, 869 mg sodium.

Ingredients:

4 slices of bread

2 eggs, beaten gently

2 ½ tbsp. butter, softened

½ tsp. salt

½ tsp. cinnamon

½ tsp. nutmeg

½ tsp. ground cloves

Maple syrup for serving

Directions:

First, preheat your Air Fryer to 350 degrees Fahrenheit.

To the side, in a medium-sized bowl, stir together the eggs, salt, cinnamon, nutmeg, and ground cloves.

Next, butter up the bread slices, and then slice the bread into French toast strips of your desired shape and size.

Next, dip the bread in the egg mixture, coating them completely.

Place the strips upon the Air Fryer. You will have to cook the strips in two batches.

After cooking them for a full two minutes, pause the Air Fryer. Then, remove the Air Fryer pan, ensuring to place the pan upon a surface that can handle it so as not to ruin your countertop.

At this time, coat the strips with a bit of butter once more, disallowing them to stick.

Return the pan to the Air Fryer, and cook the strips for another four minutes. Make sure they're cooking evenly, without burning.

After the egg is completely cooked, and the bread turns a beautiful golden brown, remove the bread from the Air Fryer. Serve the French toast sticks with a garnish of maple syrup, and enjoy.

BREAKFAST BURRITO

Recipe Makes 1 Serving.

Preparation Time: 10 minutes

Nutritional Information Per Serving: 377 calories, 23 grams carbohydrates, 21 grams fat, 26 grams protein, 1850 mg sodium.

Ingredients:

3 slices turkey breast

2 eggs

¼ sliced avocado

¼ sliced red pepper

2 tbsp. salsa

1/8 cup grated mozzarella

½ tsp. salt

½ tsp. pepper

1 tortilla

Directions:

First, beat the eggs and salt and pepper in a small bowl.

Next, pour the eggs into a non-stick pan, and place the eggs in the Air Fryer. Cook the eggs at 400 degrees Fahrenheit for five minutes.

Remove the pan, and remove the eggs from the pan as well.

Next, fill the tortilla with the egg, turkey, red pepper, avocado, cheese, and salsa. Wrap the tortilla.

Next, line your Air Fryer tray with aluminum foil. Place the burrito on the foil, and heat the burrito at 350 degrees Fahrenheit for three minutes. The tortilla should be toasted, and the cheese should be melted.

Serve with salsa.

TURKEY BACON EGG BREAKFAST SANDWICH

Recipe Makes 1 Serving.

Preparation Time: 10 minutes

Nutritional Information Per Serving: 235 calories, 26 grams carbohydrates, 6 grams fat, 16 grams protein, 1800 mg sodium.

Ingredients:

1 egg

2 slices turkey bacon

1 English muffin

Directions:

First, crack your egg into a soufflé cup, one that's oven-proof and able to survive the Air Fryer.

Next, add the soufflé cup, bacon, and the sliced English muffin in the Air Fryer.

Turn the Air Fryer up to 395 degrees Fahrenheit, and cook for six minutes.

Now, assemble your various ingredients, taking care not to burn yourself, and enjoy.

SIZZLING KETOGENIC FRITTATA FOR TWO

Recipe Makes 2 Servings.

Preparation Time: 15 minutes

Nutritional Information Per Serving: 230 calories, 2 grams carbohydrates, 18 grams fat, 15 grams protein, 936 mg sodium.

Ingredients:

2 eggs

½ Italian sausage link, chopped

3 halved cherry tomatoes

1 tbsp. olive oil

2 tbsp. grated Parmesan

½ cup chopped parsley

½ tsp. salt

½ tsp. pepper

Directions:

First, place the chopped sausage and the tomatoes in the provided baking dish, and bake in the Air Fryer for 5 minutes at 360 degrees Fahrenheit.

Next, to the side, stir together the eggs, olive oil, Parmesan, parsley, salt, and the pepper.

At this time, remove the baking dish from the Air Fryer. Add the egg mixture, and bake in the Air Fryer for a full five minutes more.

Remove the frittata from the Air Fryer, and enjoy.

OATMEAL AND RAISIN MUFFINS

Recipe Makes 6 Muffins

Preparation Time: 20 minutes

Nutritional Information Per Serving: 326 calories, 39 grams carbohydrates, 17 grams fat, 4 grams protein, 131 mg sodium.

Ingredients:

¾ cup flour

½ cup sugar

1 stick butter

½ cup rolled oats

1/3 cup raisins

2 eggs

¼ tsp. vanilla

¼ tsp. baking powder

Directions:

First, in a medium-sized bowl, cream together the sugar and the butter until soft.

Next, add the eggs, and the vanilla, beating well between each addition.

In another bowl, stir together the dry ingredients: flour, oats, raisins, and baking powder.

Next, cut the flour mixture into the butter.

At this time, place muffin liners in a muffin tray, and fill each muffin tray about ¾ of the way full. Set the muffin tin to the side.

Preheat the Air Fryer to 350 degrees Fahrenheit.

Now, place the tin in the frying basket. Bake the muffins in the preheated Air Fryer for 10 minutes.

Remove the muffins when they're browned on top, and most in the center.

GOOD MORNING MAMA POTATO HASH

Recipe Makes 4 Servings.

Preparation Time: 55 minutes

Nutritional Information Per Serving: 383 calories, 70 grams carbohydrates, 4 grams fat, 11 grams protein, 351 mg sodium.

Ingredients:

5 large potatoes

½ green pepper

1 diced onion

2 tsp. ghee

½ tsp. thyme

½ tsp. pepper

½ tsp. salt

2 eggs

Directions:

First, melt the ghee in the Air Fryer for two minutes.

At this time, dice the onions, add the onions to the Air Fryer. Dice the green pepper, and add the green pepper to the ghee and onion.

Next, wash the potatoes, and dice them into small cubes. Add the potatoes to the Air Fryer, and then douse the peppers and vegetables with the seasoning.

Next, set the timer of the Air Fryer for 30 minutes, and allow the potatoes to roast.

To the side, add a bit of ghee to a skillet. Add black pepper, allowing it to heat for a moment, before adding the eggs. Allow the eggs to cook until they're completely solid. Next, remove the skillet from the heat, and chop up the eggs. Set the eggs to the side.

After the Air Fryer beeps, add the egg to the potatoes. Cook the potatoes for another five minutes.

Serve warm, and enjoy.

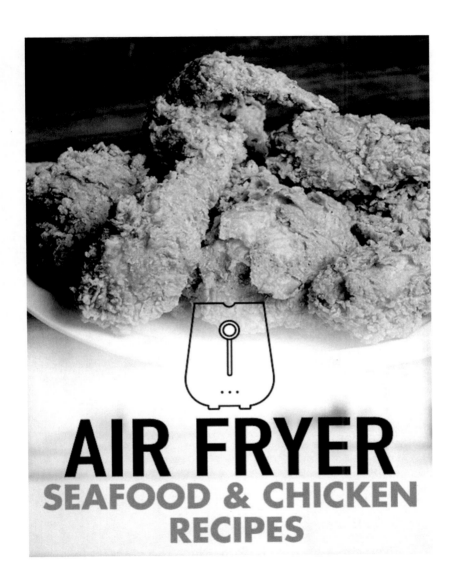

AIR FRYER
SEAFOOD & CHICKEN RECIPES

SOUTHERN "FRIED" CHICKEN

Recipe Makes 8 Servings.

Preparation Time: 3 hours pre-time, plus 30 minutes

Nutritional Information Per Serving: 306 calories, 25 grams carbohydrates, 4 grams fat, 37 grams protein, 403 mg sodium.

Ingredients:

2 pounds chicken, sliced into pieces

1 cup buttermilk

1 tsp. salt

2 cups flour

1 tsp. pepper

1 egg

Directions:

First, rinse off the chicken. Place the chicken in a sealable bag and cover the chicken with the buttermilk. Place the chicken in the refrigerator for about three hours. You can leave it in longer if you want more vibrant flavor.

Next, add flour, salt, and pepper to another sealable bag, and stir well.

Remove the chicken, and pat the chicken dry.

Crack an egg in a side dish, and dip each chicken piece in the egg before placing the chicken in the bag with the flour. Toss the chicken to coat.

Next, place the chicken pieces in the Air Fryer, and fry them for 20 minutes at 390 degrees Fahrenheit. Enjoy.

PAPRIKA MARINATED KETOGENIC CHICKEN WINGS

Recipe Makes 2 Servings.

Preparation Time: 25 minutes

Nutritional Information Per Serving: 345 calories, 1 gram carbohydrate, 6 grams fat, 65 grams protein, 1306 mg sodium.

Ingredients:

8 chicken wings

½ cup olive oil

1 tsp. hot paprika

1 tsp. salt

1 tsp. pepper

Directions:

First, pour the olive oil into a cup. Add the spices, and stir well.

Next, pour the olive oil into a large sealable bag, and add the wings. Allow the wings to marinate in the oil for about a half hour.

Next, preheat the Air Fryer to 400 degrees Fahrenheit.

Place the chicken wings on the cooking tray. Add the chicken wing tray to the Air Fryer, and cook them for 12 minutes.

Next, flip the wings and stir them slightly to avoid sticking or touching. Cook for an additional eight minutes.

Serve, and enjoy.

WHOLE ROTISSERIE CHICKEN IN THE AIR FRYER

Recipe Makes 8 Servings, depending on size of chicken (I used four pounds).

Preparation Time: One hour and five minutes.

Nutritional Information Per Serving: 342 calories, 0 grams carbohydrates, 6 grams fat, 65 grams protein, 143 mg sodium.

Ingredients:

1 cleaned rotisserie chicken (less than five pounds)
Coconut oil
Seasoned salt

Directions:

Pat the chicken dry, and then rub the coconut oil over the chicken. Season the chicken with seasoned salt.

Place the chicken in the Air Fryer, with the chicken breast down.

Cook the chicken for 30 minutes at 350 degrees Fahrenheit.

Flip the chicken over, and then cook for another 30 minutes. The inside of the chicken should be a full 165 degrees Fahrenheit.

Allow the chicken to cool for about 10 minutes prior to serving, and enjoy.

ROASTED AND EGGPLANT-STUFFED CHICKEN

Recipe Makes 2 Servings.

Preparation Time: One hour and 15 minutes

Nutritional Information Per Serving: 399 calories, 45 grams carbohydrates, 10 grams fat, 30 grams protein, 864 mg sodium.

Ingredients:

1 eggplant, medium-sized

Seeds from ½ a pomegranate

2 chicken breasts

½ cup stale, torn up pieces of sourdough bread

½ tbs. olive oil

Sprig of thyme

¼ cup flour

1 egg white

½ tsp. salt

½ tsp. pepper

Directions:

First, slice the eggplant in half, lengthwise. Add salt, and allow it to sit for 20 minutes.

Next, tear up the pieces of sourdough, and then add the sourdough to a food processor. Pulse until you've created a "crumb" with texture.

Next, add the olive oil, thyme, and a bit of salt. Pulse once more, and set the mixture to the side.

Wipe at the eggplant with a napkin or paper towel, removing water. Cook the eggplant in the Air Fryer with the cut side up. Do this for 20 minutes, at 450 degrees Fahrenheit.

Next, allow the eggplant to cool. Scoop the inside of the eggplant into a bowl, and remove all liquid.

Next, puree the eggplant's insides in a food processor, adding salt and pepper.

Add puree to a medium-sized bowl, and add the pomegranate seeds.

Next, preheat the Air Fryer to 350 degrees Fahrenheit for a full five minutes.

Next, slice the chicken breasts length-wise, creating a pocket in each one. Add the eggplant guts to the center, and then coat each chicken breast with flour.

Now, to the side, whisk together the egg white with a bit of salt. Coat each chicken breast with the egg, and then add the crumbs of sourdough to the chicken.

Add the chicken to the Air Fryer at this time, and cook the chicken for 25 minutes.

Remove the chicken, and allow it to cool for 15 minutes prior to serving.

ALL-TIME FAVORITE PALEO SWEET AND SOUR CHICKEN

Recipe Makes 4 Servings.

Preparation Time: 35 minutes.

Nutritional Information Per Serving: 440 calories, 6 grams carbohydrates, 15 grams fat, 66 grams protein, 328 mg sodium.

Ingredients:

4 chicken breasts, sliced into pieces

1 tbsp. oyster sauce

1 tsp. sesame oil

1 tsp. soy sauce

Coconut flour for coating

2 tbsp. olive oil

1 sliced green pepper

2 cubed tomatoes

1 diced onion

4 tbsp. tomato sauce, Paleo

½ cup water

1 tsp. honey

Directions:

First, mix together the oyster sauce, sesame oil, and the soy sauce in a large, sealable bag. Add the chicken to this mixture, and marinate the chicken for about 10 minutes.

Next, coat the chicken with flour.

Next, add the chicken to the Air Fryer, making sure they don't overlap. Cook the chicken at 350 degrees Fahrenheit for 10 minutes. After 10 minutes, increase the temperature to 400 degrees Fahrenheit, and cook for another 10 minutes. Next, remove the chicken from the Air Fryer. Allow them to cool.

While the chicken is cooking: to the side, heat the olive oil in a skillet. Add the garlic, and fry the garlic until browned. Add the onions, green peppers, and the tomatoes, and fry for three minutes.

Then, add the tomato sauce and the water, and bring the mixture to a boil.

Add the honey, and then stir, allowing it to simmer for five minutes. The vegetables should be soft.

Add the chicken to the skillet at this time, and stir well. Serve warm, and enjoy.

AIR FRIED ENGLISH FISH (FOR FISH AND CHIPS!)

Recipe Makes 4 Servings.

Preparation Time: 25 minutes.

Nutritional Information Per Serving: 143 calories, 4 grams carbohydrates, 7 grams fat, 14 grams protein, 395 mg sodium.

Ingredients:

2 catfish fillets

1 egg

3 slices bread, made into crumbs

½ cup tortilla chips

Juice and rind from one lemon

1 tbsp. parsley

½ tsp. salt

½ tsp. pepper

Directions:

First, slice each fish fillet in half, making four pieces. Season the fish with lemon, and set the fish to the side.

Next, grind the breadcrumbs, lemon rind, tortillas, parsley, and the salt and pepper in a food processor. Add this mixture to a large baking tray at this time.

Next, crack the egg in a small bowl, and coat each fish fillet in the egg, followed by the breadcrumbs.

Cook the fish in the Air Fryer at 350 degrees Fahrenheit. They should be crispy and fragrant.

SPICY SAMBAL CHILI FISH FILLETS

Recipe Makes 2 Servings.

Preparation Time: 30 minutes

Nutritional Information Per Serving: 478 calories, 34 grams carbohydrates, 27 grams fat, 27 grams protein, 1600 mg sodium.

Ingredients:

4 small selar fish fillets

1 tbsp. Sambal chili paste

1 tbsp. oyster sauce

½ tbsp. belachan

½ tbsp. olive oil

½ tsp. salt

1 tbsp. lime juice

Directions:

Process the chili paste, oyster sauce, belachan, olive oil, salt, and the lime juice in a food processor until smooth.

Coat the fish in the sauce, and add the fish to the Air Fryer. Fry the fish for 20 minutes at 230 degrees Fahrenheit, adjusting the temperature down to 180 degrees Fahrenheit after five minutes. About halfway through the cook time, flip the fish to the other side.

Remove the fish when they're crisp on top and fully cooked.

DELIGHTFUL LEMON FISH

Recipe Makes 4 Servings.

Preparation Time: 45 minutes.

Nutritional Information Per Serving: 187 calories, 22 grams carbohydrates, 8 grams protein, 8 grams fat, 636 mg sodium.

Ingredients:

2 fish fillets of your choice, sliced into four pieces (I used Basa fish)

1 lemon

¼ cup sugar

½ tsp. salt

2 tsp. green chili sauce

1 egg white

2 tsp. olive oil

4 tsp. cornstarch

1 tsp. red chili sauce

3 lettuce leaves

extra flour for coating

Directions:

First, slice the lemon, and place the lemon slices in a bowl.

Next, boil half cup of water in a pan, adding sugar when it begins to boil. Remove the water from the heat when the sugar dissolves.

Next, stir together the flour, salt, green chili sauce, oil, and the egg white in a medium-sized bowl, and stir well. Add 3 tbsp. water to the mixture, and stir well to create a batter.

Next, add flour to a plate.

Dip the fish in the batter, and then coat the fish with the flour on the plate.

Add the fish to the Air Fryer. Cook them at 350 degrees Fahrenheit for 20 minutes, until crispy.

Next, in a pot, add salt, cornstarch, red chili sauce, and lemon slices, stirring well. Cook the mixture until the lemon sauce begins to thicken. This will go to the side of your fish.

Remove the fish from the Air Fryer, and brush the fish with olive oil. Return the fish to the Air Fryer, and cook for an additional five minutes.

Serve the fish over the lettuce, and add the lemon sauce over the fish. Serve and enjoy!

AIR FRIED SALMON

Recipe Makes 1 Serving.

Preparation Time: 15 minutes.

Nutritional Information Per Serving: 277 calories, 0 grams carbohydrates, 15 grams fat, 34 grams protein, 1242 mg sodium.

Ingredients:

1 fillet of salmon

½ tsp. salt

1 tsp. lemon juice

1 tsp. olive oil

Directions:

Add salt, olive oil, and lemon juice to your piece of salmon, coating it to taste.

Add the salmon to the Air Fryer tray, with the skin side on the tray.

Set the timer of the Air Fryer to 10 minutes, cooking at 320 degrees Fahrenheit.

After 10 minutes, remove the salmon from the Air Fryer, and serve.

MUNCHIE COCONUT SHRIMP

Recipe Makes 3 Servings.

Preparation Time: 30 minutes.

Nutritional Information Per Serving: 385 calories, 26 grams carbohydrates, 24 grams fat, 18 grams protein, 688 mg sodium.

Ingredients:

8 shrimp, without shells and veins

½ cup shredded coconut

8 ounces coconut milk

½ tsp. cayenne pepper

½ tsp. salt

½ tsp. pepper

½ cup panko bread

1 tbsp. honey

½ tsp. powdered mustard

¼ tsp. hot sauce

½ cup marmalade, orange

Directions:

First, clean off the shrimp.

To the side, in a small bowl, stir together the coconut milk and salt and pepper. Set this mixture to the side.

In another bowl, stir together the coconut, panko, cayenne, salt, and pepper.

Next, dip the shrimp in the coconut milk, then the panko. Place the shrimp in the Air Fryer basket. Repeat this step until you've run out of shrimp.

Next, cook the shrimp in the Air Fryer for 20 minutes at 350 degrees Fahrenheit. The shrimp should be completely cooked through.

To the side, as the shrimp cook, create a sauce with the marmalade, powdered mustard, honey, and hot sauce. Stir well.

Serve the shrimp with the sauce, and enjoy.

AIR FRYER
BEEF & PORK RECIPES

SOUL WARMING ROAST BEEF

Recipe Makes 4 Servings.

Preparation Time: One hour

Nutritional Information Per Serving: 346 calories, 0 grams carbohydrates, 14 grams fat, 51 grams protein, 112 mg sodium.

Ingredients:

1.5 pounds roast beef

1 tbsp. olive oil

Salt and black pepper for seasoning

Directions:

First, preheat your Air Fryer for a full five minutes at 325 degrees Fahrenheit.

Next, add the roast to a bowl, add the oil, and rub the beef with the oil and the salt and pepper.

Add the roast to the Air Fryer at this time. Cook the roast in the Air Fryer for 30 minutes.

Next, flip your roast over, and cook it for an additional 15 minutes.

This will make a medium-cooked roast. Cook the roast for longer for a more well-done middle.

AIR FRIED BURGERS

Recipe Makes 4 Servings.

Preparation Time: 20 minutes

Nutritional Information Per Serving: 217 calories, 1 gram carbohydrate, 7 grams fat, 34 grams protein, 407 mg sodium.

Ingredients:

1 pound extra-lean ground beef

1 tbsp. Worcestershire sauce

1 tsp. Maggi seasoning sauce

½ tsp. onion powder

½ tsp. garlic powder

½ tsp. black pepper

½ tsp. salt

½ tsp. dried parsley

Directions:

First, stir together the listed seasonings in a very large bowl: Worcestershire sauce, Maggi, onion, garlic, black pepper, salt, and parsley.

Next, add the beef to this bowl. Mix, using your hand, ensuring you coat the beef well. But make sure you don't overwork the meat, as this will ultimately breed "hard" burgers.

Shape the beef into four different patties. Place the burger patties in the tray, and cook the burgers in the Air Fryer for 10 minutes at 350 degrees Fahrenheit, without turning them. Note that you can cook the burgers for longer if you want your burgers "well done".

AIR FRIED GERMAN BEEF SCHNITZEL

Recipe Makes 1 Serving.

Preparation Time: 22 minutes.

Nutritional Information Per Serving: 316 calories, 19 grams carbohydrates, 11 grams fat, 32 grams protein, 284 mg sodium.

Ingredients:

¼ cup breadcrumbs

1 egg

1 beef schnitzel, thin

1 tbsp. vegetable oil

Served with lemon

Directions:

First, preheat the Air Fryer to 350 degrees Fahrenheit.

Next, stir together the oil and the breadcrumbs. The mixture should be crumbly.

Crack an egg into a dish, and coat the schnitzel in the egg. Coat the schnitzel with the breadcrumbs, coating it completely and evenly.

Add the schnitzel to the Air Fryer, and cook for 12 minutes.

Serve with lemon, and enjoy.

AIR FRIED RIB EYE STEAK

Recipe Makes 4 Servings.

Preparation Time: 20 minutes

Nutritional Information Per Serving: 451 calories, 0 grams carbohydrates, 11 grams fat, 81 grams protein, 102 mg sodium.

Ingredients:

2 pounds rib eye steak

1 tbsp. steak rub seasoning

1 tbsp. olive oil

Direction:

Preheat the Air Fryer to 400 degrees Fahrenheit.

Next, season the steak with olive oil and the seasoning.

Place the steak in the Air Fryer basket.

Cook the steaks in the Air Fryer for 14 minutes, flipping halfway through the cook time.

After 14 minutes, remove the steak from heat, allow them to cool, slice, and serve.

WINTERTIME AIR FRIED PORK CHOPS

Recipe Makes 4 Servings.

Preparation Time: 20 minutes

Nutritional Information Per Serving: 332 calories, 11 grams carbohydrates, 21 grams fat, 21 grams protein, 800 mg sodium.

Ingredients:

4 pork loin chops

½ cup breadcrumbs

½ cup Dijon mustard

½ tsp. salt

½ tsp. pepper

½ tsp. cayenne pepper

Directions:

Preheat the Air Fryer to 400 degrees Fahrenheit.

Next, coat the pork loin chops in Dijon mustard. Note you might not use all the mustard.

Next, stir together the breadcrumbs, salt, pepper, and cayenne pepper in a medium-sized bowl. Coat each pork loin chop in the breadcrumb mixture.

Next, add the pork chops to the Air Fryer. Cook the pork chops for 16 minutes in the Air Fryer, flipping them after eight minutes.

After 16 minutes, remove the pork chops from the Air Fryer, allow them to cool, and serve.

HONEY GLAZED BBQ PORK RIBS

Recipe Makes 8 Servings.

Preparation Time: 40 minutes.

Nutritional Information Per Serving: 386 calories, 29 grams carbohydrates, 17 grams fat, 26 grams protein, 429 mg sodium.

Ingredients:

1 ¾ pounds pork ribs

½ tsp. garlic powder

½ tsp. black pepper

1 tbsp. Worcestershire sauce

1 cup BBQ sauce

½ cup honey

1 tsp. white pepper

Directions:

Stir together the garlic powder, black pepper, Worcestershire sauce, BBQ sauce, honey, and the white pepper, and add the mixture to a large, sealable bag.

Next, add the pork ribs to the large bag, and marinate them in the refrigerator for 20 minutes.

Next, preheat the Air Fryer to 350 degrees Fahrenheit for three minutes.

Place the pork ribs in the Air Fryer at this time, and cook them for 14 minutes.

Next, brush another layer of honey upon the pork ribs if you please, and serve.

SOUL AFFIRMING PALEO PORK ROAST

Recipe Makes 10 Servings.

Preparation Time: 4 hours plus 6 hours

Nutritional Information Per Serving: 369 calories, 1 gram carbohydrates, 21 grams fat, 36 grams protein, 1515 mg sodium.

Ingredients:

1 ¾ pound pork belly

1 tsp. salt

2 tsp. garlic powder

1 ½ tsp. dried rosemary

1 ½ tsp. five-spice powder

1 tsp. white pepper

Juice from ½ lemon

Directions:

First, wash the pork belly and pat it dry.

Next, boil a large pot of water, and blanch the pork belly. Do this for a full 13 minutes. Pat the pork belly dry once more. Allow the pork to air dry, in front of a fan, for about four hours at this time.

Next, stir together the salt, garlic powder, dried rosemary, five-spice powder, and white pepper to create your dry rub.

Poke holes all over your pork roast with a fork. Don't make them too deep: just surface level.

Next, turn the pork belly, and make 4 slices into the meat at about half an inch deep. At this time, add the spices to the meat with your fingers, rubbing it in well.

After you've coated the pork roast, squeeze the lemon juice over it.

Next, add the pork back to the fridge, allowing it to chill for 6 hours. This is needed to sufficiently dry out the pork.

After six hours, preheat the Air Fryer to 340 degrees Fahrenheit for five minutes.

After five minutes, add the pork belly to the Air Fryer. Cook for 30 minutes.

After 30 minutes, turn up the heat of the Air Fryer to 380 degrees Fahrenheit. Air Fry for an additional 25 minutes.

Remove the pork from heat, and allow it to cool for a little while before serving. Slice and serve.

CHINESE ROASTED PORK BELLY

Recipe Makes 4 Servings.

Preparation Time: Overnight plus one hour

Nutritional Information Per Serving: 327 calories, 0 grams carbohydrates, 8 grams fat, 59 grams protein, 129 mg sodium.

Ingredients:

2 pounds pork

Vinegar

Sea salt

Marinade Ingredients:

¼ tsp. white pepper

1 tbsp. cooking wine

½ tbsp. five spice powder

1 tsp. salt

Directions:

First, wash the pork belly. Pat it dry.

Next, rub the cooking wine over the meat of the pork, followed by white pepper, five spice powder, and the salt.

Next, place the pork belly upon a plate, uncovered, and allow it to sit overnight in the fridge.

Afterwards, remove the pork belly, and prick the belly with a fork, making many small holes all over.

Next, place the pork belly upon a sheet of aluminum foil skins side up. The aluminum foil should be big enough to wrap all the way around the pork belly. Wrap the pork belly in the aluminum foil, keeping the skin out, ensuring that the aluminum foil "walls" on all sides should be higher than the pork belly, so that it can hold the sea salt.

Next, brush the pork belly skin with the vinegar. Coat the pork belly skin with sea salt. Use enough that you can't even see the skin any more.

Preheat the Air Fryer to 350 degrees Fahrenheit.

Next, add the pork belly to the Air Fryer. Fry it for 30 minutes in the preheated Air Fryer.

Remove the pork belly, and remove the aluminum foil at this time. Scrape off all the salt and toss it.

Change the temperature of the Air Fryer to 400 degrees Fahrenheit. Add the pork belly back to the Air Fryer, and cook it for an additional 15 minutes. The skin should begin to crack.

Slice the pork belly, and serve.

AIR FRYER
VEGAN &
VEGETARIAN RECIPES

VEGAN POTATO-STUFFED BELL PEPPERS WITH INDIAN SPICES

Recipe Makes 4 Servings.

Preparation Time: 40 minutes.

Nutritional Information Per Serving: 180 calories, 30 grams carbohydrates, 5 grams fat, 5 grams protein, 575 mg sodium.

Ingredients:

4 green peppers

2 diced onions

2 cups pre-made mashed potatoes

2 tbsp. chopped coriander leaves

1 tsp. lemon juice

1 tsp. cumin seeds

½ tsp. turmeric powder

¼ tsp. chili powder

¼ tsp. Garam masala powder

½ tsp. salt

1 tbsp. olive oil

Directions:

First, heat olive oil, cumin seeds, chilies, and onions in a skillet over medium until the onions turn brown.

Add the mashed potatoes to the mixture, and reduce the heat. Next, add the turmeric, chili powder, Garam masala powder, and a bit of salt. Stir well.

Remove the mixture from the heat, and add the coriander leaves and lemon juice. Stir well. Set this mixture to the side.

At this time, cut the tops off the green peppers. Remove the insides and seeds.

Preheat the Air Fryer to 450 degrees Fahrenheit for 10 minutes.

Next, give each pepper a thin coat of oil.

Stuff each pepper with the created filling, all the way to the top.

Next, remove the Air Fryer basket carefully, and add the green peppers inside. Grill the peppers for 10 minutes.

If the green peppers are not sufficiently grilled, grill them for another five minutes. Serve the green peppers hot, and enjoy.

DELIGHTFUL PARMESAN RISOTTO

Recipe Makes 2 Servings.

Preparation Time: 30 minutes

Nutritional Information Per Serving: 263 calories, 43 grams carbohydrates, 8 grams fat, 4 grams protein, 588 mg sodium.

Ingredients:

1 tbsp. olive oil

½ cup risotto rice

1 tbsp. white wine

½ tsp. salt

1 tbsp. Parmesan cheese

2 cups vegetable stock

1 diced onion

1 diced tomato

Directions:

First, add the risotto rice to the Air Fryer, along with the olive oil, a bit of salt, and the onion.

Next, heat the risotto rice at 350 degrees Fahrenheit for two minutes. Then, add the white wine. Give it a firm stir before allowing the mixture to dissolve for two minutes. Then, add the vegetable stock.

At this time, fry the mixture for 10 minutes. Then, allow it to rest for 10 minutes, turning off the heat.

Then, allow it to cook for another 10 minutes at 350 degrees Fahrenheit once more. Add the cheese at this time, along with the tomatoes.

Then, allow the risotto to fry for another eight minutes at 350 degrees Fahrenheit. Serve, and enjoy.

VEGAN MIDDLE EASTERN FALAFEL BALLS

Recipe Makes 6 Servings.

Preparation Time: 20 minutes

Nutritional Information Per Serving: 416 calories, 56 grams carbohydrates, 15 grams fat, 17 grams protein, 26 mg sodium.

Ingredients:

1 cup rolled oats

2 tbsp. olive oil

½ cup diced onions

½ cup diced carrots

½ cup cashews, roasted and salted

2 cups chickpeas, rinsed

1 tbsp. flax meal

juice from 1 lemon

1 tsp. cumin

1 tsp. garlic powder

½ tsp. turmeric

Directions:

First, heat olive oil in a large skillet over medium heat. Cook the onions and the carrots for about eight minutes, until softened.

Next, add the cashews and the oats to a food processor. Grind them to create a meal. Then, add this to the vegetables.

Next, add the chickpeas to the fruit processor, along with the lemon juice and the soy sauce. Puree until smooth, with a few chunks.

Next, add the chickpeas to the bowl with the vegetables, and add the spices and the flax seeds. Stir well, mashing up the chickpeas that you find as you stir.

Next, create 12 falafel balls with your hands. Arrange them in one layer in the Air Fryer basket. Cook the falafel balls for 12 minutes at 370 degrees Fahrenheit, shaking them to adjust after about seven minutes.

VEGGIE CARBONARA MUSHROOM PASTA

Recipe Makes 6 Servings.

Preparation Time:

Nutritional Information Per Serving: 284 calories, 32 grams carbohydrates, 13 grams fat, 8 grams protein, 470 mg sodium.

Ingredients:

10 ounces spaghetti, cooked

3 minced garlic cloves

3 tbsp. butter

1 cup water

1 ½ cups carbonara sauce (no bacon, canned)

1 cup sliced white button mushrooms

½ tsp. salt

½ tsp. pepper

Directions:

Preheat the Air Fryer to 300 degrees Fahrenheit for five minutes.

Next, oil the sides of the Air Fryer saucepan with the butter. Add the garlic, and Air Fry the garlic for five minutes.

Next, add the mushrooms. Cook for an additional three minutes.

Next, add the sauce, water, and salt and pepper. Turn up the heat to 325 degrees Fahrenheit, and cook for an additional 18 minutes, stirring occasionally.

As you make the carbonara sauce, boil a pot of water, and add the spaghetti. Boil for about eight minutes, or until al dente.

Add the sauce over the pasta, and stir well. Garnish with parsley, if you want to.

AMERICAN LOVER'S VEGETARIAN GRILLED CHEESE

Recipe Makes 1 Serving.

Preparation Time: 10 minutes

Nutritional Information Per Serving: 377 calories, 23 grams carbohydrates, 17 grams protein, 23 grams fat, 583 mg sodium.

Ingredients:

2 slices whole wheat bread

1 ½ ounces American cheddar cheese

2 tsp. butter

Directions:

Butter the outside of both pieces of bread, and stick the cheese on the inside.

Place the grilled cheese in the Air Fryer, and cook the grilled cheese at 370 degrees Fahrenheit for a full eight minutes. Flip the sandwich after four minutes.

Enjoy with a side salad.

GORGEOUS GRILLED TOMATOES

Recipe Makes 2 Servings.

Preparation Time: 25 minutes

Nutritional Information Per Serving: 35 calories, 7 grams carbohydrates, 1 gram fat, 2 grams protein, 591 mg sodium.

Ingredients:

2 large tomatoes

1 tsp. dried basil

1 tsp. dried sage

½ tsp. salt

½ tsp. pepper

Directions:

First, slice each tomato in half.

Sprinkle the halves with black pepper and herbs.

Place the tomato halves in the Air Fry top tray with the cut side up.

Fry the tomatoes at 320 degrees Fahrenheit for 20 minutes, without preheating.

Remove the tomatoes, and serve warm. Enjoy.

AMAZING AIR FRIED TOFU BITES

Recipe Makes 4 Servings.

Preparation Time: 55 minutes

Nutritional Information Per Serving: 102 calories, 4 grams carbohydrates, 8 grams protein, 6 grams fat, 469 mg sodium.

Ingredients:

14 ounce block of tofu, sliced into one-inch bite-sized pieces

2 tbsp. soy sauce

2 tsp. toasted sesame oil

1 tsp. seasoned rice vinegar

1 tbsp. cornstarch

Directions:

Slice the tofu, and toss the tofu in a large bowl with the soy sauce, vinegar, and the oil. Allow the tofu to marinate for 30 minutes.

Next, toss the tofu with the cornstarch. Add the tofu to the Air Fryer, and cook the tofu for 20 minutes at 370 degrees Fahrenheit.

Serve the tofu bites with a sauce of your choice, and enjoy.

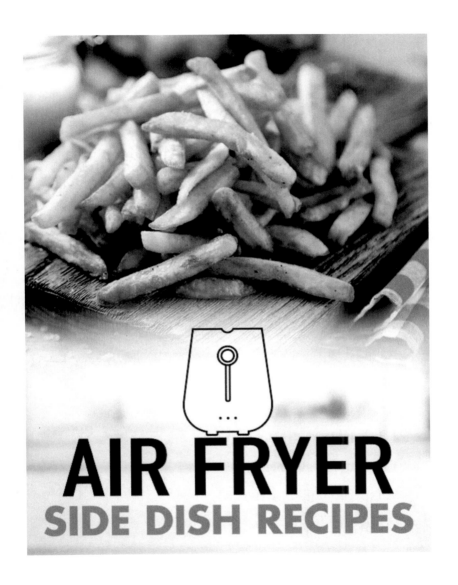

AIR FRYER
SIDE DISH RECIPES

INDIAN CHEESE BALLS

Recipe Makes 3 Servings.

Preparation Time: 25 minutes.

Nutritional Information Per Serving: 202 calories, 15 grams carbohydrates, 8 grams fat, 16 grams protein, 818 mg sodium.

Ingredients:

1 cup Paneer cottage cheese

½ cup cheese cubes

2 tbsp. flour

1 tbsp. corn flour

2 diced onions

1 diced green chili

1 inch diced ginger piece

½ tsp. red chili powder

½ tsp. salt

Directions:

First, stir together the cottage cheese, flour, corn flour, onions, green chili, ginger, red chili powder, and the salt until completely combined. Form approximately one inch balls until you have no mixture left.

Next, add cheese cubes to the inside of the cottage cheese balls, ensuring they're completely covered by the other mixture by sealing the edges. Repeat this process until you're finished.

Place the balls in the Air Fryer and bake at 400 degrees Fahrenheit for 15 minutes. Serve warm, and enjoy.

DOWN HOME BAKED POTATO

Recipe Makes 3 Servings.

Preparation Time: 45 minutes

Nutritional Information Per Serving: 336 calories, 58 grams carbohydrates, 10 grams fat, 6 grams protein, 798 mg sodium.

Ingredients:

3 large russet baking potatoes

2 tbsp. olive oil

1 tsp. parsley

1 tsp. garlic

1 tsp. salt

Directions:

First, scrub your potatoes, and then create tiny holes with your fork around all the potatoes.

Next, sprinkle them with salt and olive oil, along with the parsley and garlic.

After you've coated them, place the potatoes in the Air Fryer. Cook them on 395 degrees Fahrenheit in the Air Fryer for 40 minutes, until the potatoes are tender.

Top with your favorite ingredients, and enjoy.

IRRESISTIBLE BRUSSELS SPROUTS

Recipe makes 4 Servings.

Preparation Time: 45 minutes.

Nutritional Information Per Serving: 59 calories, 10 grams carbohydrates, 1 gram fat, 4 grams protein, 610 mg sodium.

Ingredients:

1 pound Brussels sprouts

1 tsp. salt

4 tsp. olive oil

Directions:

Rinse and halve each of the Brussels sprouts. Toss the Brussels sprouts with olive oil and salt.

Next, preheat the Air Fryer to 390 degrees Fahrenheit. Add the sprouts to the Air Fryer and cook them for 15 minutes. Every few minutes, shake the sprouts to ensure they don't stick.

Remove the sprouts from the heat when they're tender, with caramelized outsides.

Serve, and enjoy.

AIR FRIED EGGPLANT CHIPS

Recipe Makes 2 Servings.

Preparation Time:

Nutritional Information Per Serving: 57 calories, 13 grams carbohydrates, 1 gram fat, 3 grams protein, 524 mg sodium.

Ingredients:

1 large eggplant

Olive oil

Salt

Directions:

Slice the eggplant into very thin "chips." Place them in a medium-sized bowl, and sprinkle them with olive oil and salt. Coat them completely, and then place them in the Air Fryer.

Turn up the Air Fryer to 400 degrees Fahrenheit, and cook for five minutes. Shake them well, and then cook for another five minutes.

Sprinkle with a little more sea salt, and serve.

PALEO FAUX-FRIED RICE

Recipe Makes 8 Servings.

Preparation Time: 40 minutes

Nutritional Information Per Serving: 120 calories, 18 grams carbohydrates, 3 grams fat, 6 grams protein, 598 mg sodium.

Ingredients:

1 large head of cauliflower

1 tbsp. sesame oil

5 tbsp. soy sauce

5 minced garlic cloves

1 tbsp. minced ginger

1 cup peas

8 ounces water chestnuts, chopped

16 ounces mushrooms

2 eggs

Juice from ½ a lemon

Directions:

First, stir together the sesame oil, soy sauce, garlic, ginger, and the lemon juice.

Next, chop the cauliflower, and then process the cauliflower in a food processor. Add this to the lemon juice mixture and stir well.

Next, add the water chestnuts, and stir.

Next, add this mixture to the Air Fryer, and cook for 20 minutes at 350 degrees Fahrenheit.

After 20 minutes, add the peas, and then the mushrooms. Cook for another 15 minutes.

To the side, cook the eggs in a skillet to create a firm omelet. Chop the omelet, and then add the egg to the rice mixture. Cook for another five minutes.

Serve warm, and enjoy.

PALEO SWEET POTATO FRIES

Recipe Makes 5 Servings.

Preparation Time: 35 minutes.

Nutritional Information Per Serving: 142 calories, 33 grams carbohydrates, 1 gram fat, 1 gram protein, 11 mg sodium.

Ingredients:

2 large sweet potatoes

1 tbsp. olive oil

Salt

Pepper

Directions:

First, wash the sweet potatoes, and peel them.

Slice the potatoes into fries. Add a tbsp. of olive oil to a bowl, and then toss the fries in the bowl until completely coated.

Next, add the fries to the Air Fryer, and cook at 320 degrees Fahrenheit for 15 minutes.

Remove the fries, and add them back to a large bowl. Toss them with salt and pepper, and then move them back to the Air Fryer. Raise the temperature to 350 degrees Fahrenheit, and cook for an additional five minutes.

Next, toss the fries once more. Return the fries to the Air Fryer, still at 350 degrees Fahrenheit. Roast for another five minutes, and then serve warm.

CROQUETTES FILLED WITH CHEDDAR AND BACON

Recipe Makes 6 Servings.

Preparation Time: 14 minutes

Nutritional Information Per Serving: 591 calories, 10 grams carbohydrates, 44 grams fat, 36 grams protein, 1711 mg sodium.

Ingredients:

1 pound sliced bacon at room temperature

1 pound block of sharp cheddar cheese

2 beaten eggs

2 tbsp. olive oil

1 cup flour

½ cup breadcrumbs, seasoned

Directions:

First, slice up the cheddar block into eight portions, each about an inch by two inches long.

Next, wrap two slices of bacon around each piece of cheddar. Enclose it as well as you can, and then trim off the fat.

Now, place these bacon cheddar pieces in the freezer for five minutes. Don't allow them to freeze!

Next, preheat the Air Fryer to 390 degrees Fahrenheit.

To the side, stir together the breadcrumbs and the oil. Stir until the mixture is crumbly.

At this time, crack the egg in a small bowl, and then add flour to a separate dish. Dip the cheddar bacon balls in the flour, then the egg, and then the breadcrumbs.

Place the created bites in the Air Fryer basket, and cook them for eight minutes. They should be golden brown.

AIR FRIED SEASONED FRENCH FRIES

Recipe Makes 4 Servings.

Preparation Time: 30 minutes plus 50 minutes

Nutritional Information Per Serving: 138 calories, 31 grams carbohydrates, 1 gram fat, 4 grams fat, 12 mg sodium.

Ingredients:

2 large russet potatoes, peeled and sliced into fries

1 tbsp. olive oil

Garlic herb French fry seasoning

Directions:

Place the potatoes in a large bowl, and cover the potatoes with water. Allow the fries to soak for a full 30 minutes.

At this time, preheat the Air Fryer to 360 degrees Fahrenheit.

Next, add half of the fries to the Air Fryer, and cook them for five minutes. Remove the fries, and stir them with tongs.

Next, change the temperature of the Air Fryer to 390 degrees Fahrenheit, and return the fries to the Air Fryer. Cook until they're golden brown. This should take about 15 minutes more. Make sure that you stir and toss them every five or 10 minutes so that they don't stick together.

After they're cooked, remove them and pour them into a large bowl, where you can toss them in the seasoning.

Return the Air Fryer temperature to 360 degrees Fahrenheit, and repeat with the remaining fries. Serve, and enjoy.

DELIGHTFUL ZUCCHINI FRIES

Recipe Makes 4 Servings.

Preparation Time: 45 minutes

Nutritional Information Per Serving: 79 calories, 13 grams carbohydrates, 1 gram fat, 5 grams protein, 125 mg sodium.

Ingredients:

2 zucchinis, sliced into fries

½ cup panko crumbs

1/3 cup grated Parmesan

½ tsp. oregano

½ tsp. cayenne pepper

2 egg whites

Directions:

First, stir together the cheese, spices, and the panko crumbs in a medium-sized bowl.

Slice the zucchini.

Next, add the egg whites to a small bowl. Pour the crumb mixture upon a small plate.

Coat the zucchini in the egg white, and then coat them with the crumb mixture.

Add the zucchini fries to the Air Fryer, and cook them for seven minutes at 350 degrees Fahrenheit. After seven minutes, flip the zucchini fries, and then cook them for an additional seven minutes.

Serve them warm, and enjoy.

AIR FRYER
DESSERT RECIPES

NEVER BETTER APPLE PIE PASTRIES

Recipe Makes 10 Servings.

Preparation Time: 28 minutes

Nutritional Information Per Serving: 386 calories, 30 grams carbohydrates, 25 grams fat, 2 grams protein, 286 mg sodium.

Ingredients:

1 tbsp. lemon juice

3 ½ medium apples, sliced and chopped

2 tbsp. flour

2 tsp. cinnamon

1 tsp. nutmeg

½ tsp. cloves, ground

10 sheets filo pastry

1 cup melted butter

2 tsp. sugar

Directions:

First, thaw the filo pastry completely.

Next, stir together the lemon juice, apples, sugar, flour, and all the spices in a large bowl.

To the side, unroll the filo pastry. As you work with filo pastry, you must ensure it doesn't lose any of its dampness. It dries out quickly, so cover it with a tea towel as you work.

Next, gently brush each of the pieces of filo pastry with butter, and place about a third of a cup of the apple spice mixture in the center of the filo pastry. This should be approximately two inches from the bottom of the filo pastry sheet.

Next, fold the bottom of the filo up over the apple and spice filling. Fold the sides of the pastry over the apple, and then continue to fold it up as if you were folding a flag. As you fold, continue to brush the filo pastry with butter.

Next, fill the rest of the filo pastries.

Cook the filled filo pastries in the Air Fryer at 315 degrees Fahrenheit for eight minutes each. Ensure you check on the apple pastries after about four minutes. This way, you don't run the risk of burning them and ruining your hard work.

Cook until the apples are soft and the filo pastry is crisp and tan. Cool the pastries, but serve while still warm.

AIR FRIED BANANA CHIPS

Recipe Makes 4 Servings.

Preparation Time: 12 minutes.

Nutritional Information Per Serving: 105 calories, 26 grams carbohydrates, 1 gram fat, 1 gram protein, 1 mg sodium.

Ingredients:

4 raw bananas

½ tsp. black pepper

½ tsp. salt

½ tsp. oil for frying

Directions:

First, peel the bananas. Slice each banana into very thin chips, and then add salt and pepper to the chips, along with a bit of oil.

Place the chips in the Air Fryer, and allow the chips to cook for 10 minutes at 350 degrees Fahrenheit.

Allow them to cool, and enjoy as a sweet snack.

AIR BAKED CHOCOLATE CAKE

Recipe Makes 4 Servings.

Preparation Time: 45 minutes

Nutritional Information Per Serving: 362 calories, 50 grams carbohydrates, 16 grams fat, 5 grams protein, 649 mg sodium.

Ingredients:

1 cup brown sugar

½ cup flour

¼ cup cocoa powder

1 tsp. baking powder

1 tsp. baking soda

½ tsp. salt

1 egg

½ cup milk

1 tsp. vanilla

¼ cup vegetable oil

½ cup hot water

Directions:

First, preheat the Air Fryer to 350 degrees Fahrenheit for five minutes.

Next, stir together the dry ingredients, including the brown sugar, flour, cocoa powder, baking powder, baking soda, and the salt.

Next, add the milk, egg, oil, and vanilla, stirring well between each addition.

Add the hot water last, stirring well to make an even mixture.

Pour the mixture into the baking pan, and then cover the baking pan with foil. Poke a few holes into the foil with a fork.

Place the baking tray in the Air Fryer basket, and adjust the temperature down to 325 degrees Fahrenheit. Bake for 35 minutes.

After 35 minutes, remove the foil. Bake for another 10 minutes, until a fork dipped into the center comes out clean.

Allow the chocolate cake to cool for about 10 minutes before removing it from the pan, and enjoy this very moist, delightful cake.

LEMON CHEESECAKE

Recipe Makes 6 Servings.

Preparation Time: 45 minutes

Nutritional Information Per Serving: 345 calories, 21 grams carbohydrates, 25 grams fat, 8 grams protein, 231 mg sodium.

Ingredients:

1 ¾ cups cream cheese

½ cup sugar

1 tsp. vanilla

Juice from one lemon

Zest from one lemon

3 eggs

3 tbsp. corn flour

Directions:

First, preheat the Air Fryer to 325 degrees Fahrenheit for 10 minutes.

To the side, stir together the cream cheese, vanilla, sugar, and the lemon juice until they're well combined and smooth.

Next, add the eggs one at a time, stirring in between.

Next, add the corn flour, and stir well.

At this time, pour the mixture into the oven dish, and place the dish into the Air Fryer's basket.

Bake the cheesecake for 35 minutes, at 325 degrees Fahrenheit.

After 35 minutes, remove the cheesecake, and allow it to cool. Place the cheesecake in the fridge to chill completely, and then serve.

AIR FRYER DONUTS

Recipe Makes 4 Servings.

Preparation Time: 25 minutes

Nutritional Information Per Serving: 347 calories, 46 grams carbohydrates, 17 grams fat, 3 grams protein, 130 mg sodium.

Ingredients:

1 cup self-raising flour

½ cup sugar

½ cup brown sugar

½ cup whole milk

1 tsp. baking powder

3 tbsp. butter

1 egg

For the icing:

½ cup butter

¾ cup icing sugar

½ tsp. pink food coloring (optional)

1/3 cup blended strawberries, fresh

1 tbsp. whipped cream

Directions:

First, preheat the Air Fryer to 350 degrees Fahrenheit.

Next, stir together the flour, sugar, brown sugar, butter, milk, egg and the baking powder. Make sure you don't over mix.

Next, cut the donuts with a donut-cutter to remove the inner holes.

Next, add donuts to a baking sheet, and cook the donuts in the Air Fryer for 15 minutes.

Allow them to cool for five minutes. At this time, make the icing.

Cream together the sugar and the butter, until it's smooth.

Add the whipped cream, the strawberries, and the food coloring. Mix well.

After the donuts cool, add the frosting, and enjoy.

AIR FRIED FALL TIME SWEET POTATO PIE

Recipe Makes 10 Servings

Preparation Time: Two hours and 40 minutes

Nutritional Information Per Serving: 347 calories, 31 grams carbohydrates, 5 grams protein, 22 grams fat, 393 mg sodium.

Pie Crust Ingredients (for 9-inch crust):

2 ½ cups all-purpose flour

1 cup butter, cut into small cubes

1 tsp. sugar

1 tsp. salt

8 tbsp. water

Ingredients:

1 large sweet potato

1 tsp. olive oil

flour for the workspace

2 eggs

¼ cup heavy cream

2 tbsp. maple syrup

1 tbsp. brown sugar

1 tsp. vanilla

1 tbsp. melted butter

½ tsp. nutmeg

½ tsp. cinnamon

Directions:

First, prepare your pie crust.

Add the flour, sugar, and salt to a large food processor bowl, and pulse to mix. Add half the butter cubes, and pulse until crumbly, before adding the rest of the butter. Pulse eight times. The largest pieces of the butter should be about a centimeter across.

Add about half of the water to the mixture, and pulse again. Then, add the rest of the water, just one tablespoon at a time, and pulse in between. The dough should begin to maintain its structure.

Empty the dough from the food processor upon a cutting board covered with flour. Press it with the palm of your hand, making sure you don't knead too much. This will toughen the dough.

Create a small disk from the dough, and refrigerate it for about an hour before use.

Next, place the dough upon your cutting board, and roll it into a nine-inch crust, adding flour to prevent sticking.

Now, it's time to make your pie.

First, rub the sweet potato with the olive oil, evenly coating it. Add the sweet potato to the Air Fryer, and close it. Cook the sweet potato at 400 degrees Fahrenheit for 30 minutes. After 30 minutes, the sweet potato should be tender. Remove it from the fryer, and then allow it to cool for a full 25 minutes. Remove the skin, and mash it in a medium-sized bowl.

As you cook the sweet potato, add the prepared pie crust to the nine-inch pie pan. Fold the edges over the rim of the pie pan, crimping it for decoration.

Afterwards, mash the potato with the eggs, cream, sugar, maple syrup, butter, salt, vanilla, cinnamon, and nutmeg. Stir well to combine completely.

Next, pour the sweet potato into the pie pan, over the crust, and add the pie pan to the Air Fryer.

Set the temperature of the Air Fryer to 320 degrees Fahrenheit. Cook the pie for 30 minutes, until the pie is set and the crust is golden.

At this time, remove the pie pan from the Air Fryer. Let the pie cool down for 25 minutes, and serve the pie with whipped cream for best results.

Conclusion

This cookbook, is your one-stop shop to using this truly revolutionary appliance. With safety, cleaning, and user tips in hand, you can proceed to some of the most delightful recipes, including desserts, chicken, breakfast, beef, sides, and vegetarian dishes, to follow your diet plans, lose weight, and stick to your ever-hectic schedule. We hope you enjoy the recipes!

Printed in France by Amazon
Brétigny-sur-Orge, FR

10844893R00077